on second thought

on second thought

Jason J. Humphreys

For truth seekers everywhere

Contents

Rain Is a Healing

the complaints
the sighs
the heaving against
the heavenly skies

"it's raining again..."
the weatherman spouts
his spin
"a 'nice' weekend in store
with sun and a high
of 21"

and we gulp down
the tripe since we can't
plan without that star

yet seeing those drops
hitting the still surface
of this boggy river
(a pianist tickling the ivories)
in the autumnal time...

observing rivulets
eroding their path
down my driveway
carrying the silt...

standing in the tepid drink
refreshed
refashioned
reborn...

hence this cloud that follows
like some stray mongrel
that hangs overhead
like 40 million black flies
fills me

drains me

moves me to accomplish
unimaginable things
yet leaves a smothering
stillness

but I don't stop

I walk onward
jumping in every puddle
soaked to the soul
with love gushing from
my navel like a
painless bloody nose
(I've yet to lose a pint)
while impressions like
soapstone carvings burst forth
where my drops hit the ground
(all marked down)

and I see Mom again
working in her garden
and Dad with a fishing rod
and a steel-head trout
and blackberry brambles
leaving welts
and four-litre ice cream buckets
filled with blueberry fields
and the smell of old man's beard
and heady loam and moss
and gurgling springtime springs
and that perfect duck drawing
I spent all school noon hour at
(because I just had to)...

and my great oak friend
who carried me when I cried

then I ask (out loud?)
"is this what it means
to survive the Flood?"

my pet drenches me
again
as I'm grinning stupidly
again
from temple to temple
while screaming
"come on!
is that all you can do?!"

I'm pelted
pounded
pushed
beaten
kicked
bitten
but there's
no pain
for as I look up
I see my face...

I'm the cloud
drenching me
washing me

and I'm clean

Stones

they were in my pocket as I sat
nestled in that craggy throne
while overlooking a throng
of sea-washed remnants
all wailing "Mama!"

how intently I listened
to the persistent thrumming -
the heartbeat of the world -
without voices to tempt me
out of my shadowy cocoon

then minutes translated into hours
into...(you know the progression)
and I became my own timepiece -
a towering townless clock

like an actor in a Greek comedy
the shore took on appearances
of crowded concerts and
packed-out football stadiums
filled with fans whipped into
a frenzied meringue

and I'm teleported to that
ancient altar where Titans
fought and railed against each other
and their fate was a Facebook page
where you had the freedom to click like
or not

even now my fingers skitter
over those long forgotten
surfaces and textures as if
Casimir forces are acting
wonderfully upon me
through M-theory

how is it that just by feel
I'm on Africa's west coast
millions of years ago
tasting its molten cradle?

ahhhhh... Pangaea...
I've missed you
longed for you
though not even knowing
you

your children
still spin yarns -
your sacred gift
our eternal heritage

Snapshot

click...

I recoil from a flash burned retina
like a hot pin shoved into my heel
and the image clings like a dryer sheet
(unrelenting grip)

as the dusty light clears incrementally
my eyes fall on you and your mask
has changed towards me
alone

have you left me too?
for I shudder to think of the ping
of snapping threads unravelling
unwinding

so, then, it's true?
the cord's cut?
the connection's gone?
the bridge has finally crumbled?

I'm befuddled...
winning words fail to coalesce
and roll off my tongue like buttery taffy
or maple sugar

that nanomoment
(you know...
the finite one with no
extended warranty
much like Hawking radiation
blipping in and out?)
has flown by

no resurrection
no resurfacing
I've lost you

forever...

Storm Chasers

if I would see this thing through
I'd mouth my future self to you
while you'd spew loving hate to me
and we'd sit there as if each of us
were in a corner of a boxing ring
with useless and deformed guards
at the end of round two while our
angelic demons told us what to do

I can't stand the man I'm pregnant with
who can body slam without a thought
and can't handle an egg with finesse -
I can only make omelettes that burn
all the way down

now, if I was schooled in Paris
crêpes would be easy
and I'd coat them with lemon juice,
icing sugar, and toasted almond slices
instead of chilies, scotch bonnets,
and ghost peppers
(seeds and all)

your pools are filling up to wash
you out by your own salty apologies
with nostrils sky raised and flaring
and the hurricane we gave birth to
hasn't been downgraded by the NHC
for it needs to make landfall to lose
steam
yet landfall creates
destruction
(sometimes death)

I'm afraid of you and me and
I'm fearful of me and you for
so forcefully unstoppable are we
that shingles fly off like frisbees in

summer gales and straw pierces
brick walls and cars are piled like
failed domino competitions
and vertical becomes horizontal
and diagonal
and polymorphic
and delusional

then someone (not me, not you)
takes the kettle off of the stove
'cause it's almost bone dry
the carpet's warmed in
certain ways by sunlight
then we get the dumbest
looks on our faces while
we laugh and ask each other
"what just happened?"

Core

okay...

now that I've changed
who am I?
playdough? -
since clay is a form
of moldable art
turned into crackpots?

what of the undulating
center of the earth?

what would happen if it morphed
from nickel-iron to nickel-cobalt?
would said shift -
said transmogrification -
affect rotational period
magnetic field strength
gravitational pull
and the like?

I know, I know,
change is often a necessary
and uncomfortable evil
but then ripples make waves
and identity thefts create debts
and knowing me is not knowing

do you know me
anymore
do you love me
for who I am
(not who I was)
anymore

if these all or nothing
proposals
are to fit my all or nothing

moods
do I transition like
a star
all the way from hydrogen
to iron
which results in nothing but
implosion
as what surrounds me gets
sucked into this unavoidable
mass grave that I didn't mean
to make?

or perhaps one where
there's no internal pressure
to offset gravitation
the lack of resistance results in
explosion -
a multi-directional obliteration
of everything
(everyone)
for light years around

in that galactic flashbulb moment -
that all or nothing modification
of everything
(everyone) -
where am I now?

gone?

Sprig

watercolour studies make for
drowning in rosemary-scented
jellies while drinking sage

a strawberry Twizzler droops
(as if I'd imitate the addicted)
from my closefisted grip
for I don't feel like sharing
the spark of my kid brain

it's anomalous to me how
spring-infused tips bid
welcome to the plucky
four-footed (and feathered) ones -
those that tenderly whisper
'eat me'

and I'm inspired to nip in the bud
that weedy and tendril train
before my loom has woven
the skein integrally

since wool gathering gives way to carding
I leave the spinning (out of control)
to other toilers -
the ones that step in time to the
oblivious toroidal dances

syncopation
out-of-phase
off beat -
these truisms and watermarks
lead to ridicule and slander
but not to personal shame

therefore, is what you are growing
in your heart-soil worth the wait?

Lies

at every turn I encounter you;
your obscenities,
your contemptuous sneers,
your prowling greed

your restless and unsatisfied father
fashioned you out of hubris,
an unnatural wish,
and a burning hatred

unabated you grew bloated and disfigured
until your roots fingered and weaved through
every weakness
every crack

I'm calling you out
O method actor
high born
high minded
high handed

your threads are now woven
so deeply
so deftly
into the warp and woof
of human fabric
would your erasure
result in the other's?

'I don't understand,' say you
'that can't be,' say you
'you don't know of what you speak,'
say you

okay then...

fine...

shall we take a brief jaunt through
this photo album and
engage in a forensic study of it
together?
will that convince you,
snuffing out your suspicions?

ah! here's the first entry...

this black and white from six millennia ago
 - don't touch it! -
(you can still make out the seed husk
see?... there... in the corner)
the soil was perfect
the conditions were ripe

'you positively will not die!'
but my mother did
as did those in super typhoon Haiyan
and the ones in palliative care

and the schoolteacher down the road
the one who never got a cold
it happened in her sleep
she was 127 years old
(so young)

moving on
notice this slideshow...

(children have blurred vision
in distinguishing fact from fiction
so parents need precision
in using the art of diction)

father: look at what Santa brought you!
son: a new bike! and just the one I wanted!
five years later...
father: look at what Santa brought you!
son: Dad... I know it was you...
ten years later...
father: why did you lie to me?

son: why so surprised? I learned it from you.

fibbing – I mean flipping – to the next page...

a beautiful couple -
their wedding day
their honeymoon
their first house
their various anniversaries
Roman holidays
and family reunions

in all of these pictures
do you notice something very odd?
'the woman tapping on his shoulder?'
exactly! do you know what else is
peculiar about this series?
'that woman wasn't there when the photos
were taken?'
very good! now here is the last photo
in this sequence
what do you see?
'strange...? his wife is now holding hands
with a life size wax replica of him while
he is tapping the other woman's shoulder
at her wedding'
and guess what?
'he wasn't there when the photo was taken?'
wonderful! you're really getting the hang of this
'I still don't understand the meaning'
that's alright... it takes time...

now here is a politician:
'I misquoted myself.'
a clergyman:
'fight for God and country!'
a salesman:
'this is the last car you'll ever need. guaranteed!'
shall I continue
ad infinitum?

'well, then, truth is subjective.'

click...
perfect! another one for the album
this one really catches that moment of
facial rationalization
what do you think?

The Gentleman's Way

a cravat
a kerchief
a pocket watch
a walking cane
a slight bow
a dignified gait -
chivalrous accoutrements

the offered hand
the measured word
the tip of the hat
the drying of others' tears
the token of admiration -
not superfluous garnish
but flavourful spice
a sweetening salt

those times birthed a noble attitude
a certain grace in humility
and yet a confident air
denoting caring gestures
a responsibility through example

it was an awakening
an acute awareness
that inherited station
and wealth
though not stolen from others
belonged to others
had to be used for others
was for the good of others

such conventions of kingly selflessness
where are they now?
where are those Atlantean moral giants
and their marbled halls of power?

it's Oak Island's treasure

it's the Titanic
it's Elysium
Shangri-La
and Shangdu
in one

it's history
a fable
it's mystery
a loss

Censor

heavily redacted files
described as news with
'the opinions expressed in this article are not
necessarily those of this
company and its affiliates'

disclaimer (n.):
I don't accept responsibility
I pass the buck

because of peer (fear) pressure
I'll give you the floor but
I'll stand in the shadows
to black out - blot out -
your thoughts

there is courage
(blindness) in
anonymity
but don't ask for a
face to face or tête-à-tête
else I'll mask and
double filter myself

if there's a following
the most incendiary riposte
is employed
but to stand outside the circle...

with stentorian utterances
swirling tornado-like
and the bullets hone in
on my unique signature

does freedom of speech
mean freedom to say
whatever
whenever

however
mean tongue wagging
gossiping
slandering
backbiting?

why then slap on
the following label:
'how's my driving?'

give and take
yes?
crest meets trough?
peace
crest meets crest?
war
(naturally inverted)

at the far side
if truth creates offence
and bias creates friends
what should be sacrificed?

how should I lance your boil
dress your wound
excise that gangrenous limb
when my choice is sword or
scalpel?

but touting
'go with the flow'
'don't rock the boat'
'acceptance and tolerance'
'be diplomatic' -
mere excusing
sheer recusing

we're not conflict seekers
for conflict is the effect
of standing up and
standing out
for the cause of

truth

since two bodies (of thought)
are not able to occupy
the same space at
the same time

remember Enoch...

Evolution of a Bully

on the playground
(in the classroom)
control coalesces
groups form around
a central nucleus

shoved
humiliated
mocked
lunch money stolen
homework slave

must struggle
adapt
camouflage
survive

from the homogeneous soup
of the young
and innocent
distinct forms arise
clash
evolutionary pressure's applied
and the psychology goes
mainstream

your failure
(refusal)
to evolve
to conform
to accept
their branding of
enlightenment
leads to the strong
powerful
warlike
influential
raining down on you

like a mass extinction event
and now...

groups of experts form
around a central nucleus

we are toilet dunked
locked in lockers
upended in trash bins
shoved into fences
(social) media shamed and
force-fed dimwitted diatribe
(tasteless porridge)
so we take ourselves out of
the equation
defying such elitism

via your lingua universalis
you adamantly stake claim
on Mars' Hill for your
bidirectional pursuit and
eschewing of truth

pregnant with aggrandizing
you've birthed an
extremist dogma
(the cult of Janus)
with missionaries spreading
soldiers enforcing

this arrogant flood
drowns (out!) sincerity

do you dare (silence!)
the discipline of so-called
objectivity?

must Mr. Galilei (recant!) again,
and with heavy heart,
look into the infinite dark,
as he weeps softly
(ever so softly)

"I'm sorry..."
lest someone hears?

X Marks the Flaw

do you recollect when
you weren't permitted
a red pen in school?
(perhaps you know why
maybe not)

when that math test
or spelling quiz
came back to you in
your cubby hole
the dull and painful
realization was made
clear

amidst HB striations and
blue ink dobs
you saw 'it' -

not the nine check marks
only the one red X
which sat over your answer
like a kudu in the cross-hairs
of a poacher
or an important voice in a
sniper's sights

did you sit there
patting yourself on the back
congratulating yourself on
how well you actually did
how much of an accomplishment
you achieved
how much of an affirmation this was
an authority figure's approving nod
personal validation reached?

or were they obscured
and become nonentities

like an out-of-focus shot with
too much white in the white balance
or washed out for too much sunlight
and 'it' took up the entire foreground?

a horrible name you couldn't speak
lest it transmute into an alchemical curse
to bleach your history
a scorch mark on your favourite silk tie
a fixed point in space time
where the collapsed wave function
and your triune self meet

this half-emptying of joy
this robbing of success
extortion of satisfaction
feast of suffering
is a kiln for baking
crumbly low grade bricks
for building straw houses

on this very day
all we seek
is that lone blackhead
hair out of place
the saucy drip on our sleeve

and since the ideal is a foreign tongue
we look to others' devices and say
'perfect!'
until...

we see that lone blackhead
hair out of place
the saucy drip on the sleeve

and again we take comfort in
this half-emptying of joy
this robbing of success
extortion of satisfaction
feast of suffering
and our straw house

is burned up by gale-force winds
with no grain in sight

just a gilded paper
from the second grade
on the fridge
(your mom put it there)
with nine checks
and one red X on
question number two:
'what is one minus one?'
your answer?

minus one

La Mort des Arbres

boneyard -
my reactionary thought
(elegy)
for the Lovecraft panorama
browbeating the pump
that pauses;
a respectful silence
(take a deep breath)

I give my water back
with hopes that palpable
sorrow
(loss)
slick as Bunker C
resurrects

yet bitterness is my cup
stale coffee grounds
no moisture
no pleasure

no pleasure
with execution
carried out
because the governor
is still sawing logs
waiting for dismemberment
to keep him warm
light his way

(it's genocide honouring
luxury
unlike slandered beasts
taking only what's needed)

and unsatisfied with his
accoutrements
he lines his bed with more

skeletons

unburied
flayed
beheaded
now useful
(unlike before...)

table replacing table
(nothing wrong)
chairs replace chairs
(nothing wrong)
bureau replacing bureau
(nothing wrong)
armoire replaces armoire
(still nothing wrong)

there's no (future) life on Mars

Moses In the Garden

this piece of slate
for perspective's sake
spoke to me like
Sinai's flagstones fused

imagining his face
he descends
emitting light
joyfully radiant
for glimpsing the
ancient glory
for bearing tradition's
betterment

a people promising
yet still failing
because they
(and humanity's greater
majority)
choose to forget

a legalistic and stony heart
knows only of law
technicality
rules
dos
don'ts
while building unscalable
walls
refusing to see though
opacity

the living heart
beating heart
breathing heart
filled with blood
is wider in scope
while gazing into

principle's infinite
gesture and domain

therefore
are you astonished
that the headstrong
stubborn
proud
can only stand in one place
immovable
for (what they think are)
their rights
just as granite mounts
refuse to budge?

but living hearts
beating hearts
breathing hearts
filled with blood
refuse to build walls
they dismantle and
repurpose them
to bridge divide and
chasm
for they won't be contained
nor constrained

these hearts of faith
bend and flex
yet submit
obey

acquiescing to higher laws
not only knowing but
accepting evidence
for things both visible and
invisible

just like the shepherd with
his staff

The Vicissitudes of Crashing

O incessant pounding!
you beautiful distraction -
a flood tide of worrisome questions
sine and cosine alteration
while the talented spinster
with soap shard marking
hand-me-downs
(not too threadbare)
handles her shears fluidly

cut... slash... snip...
cut... slash... snip...
cut... slash... snip...

and milk-sop stained cloth
with strained prunes, mashed carrots,
and peas
falls in strands with a certain finality
of change in the barber's chair
(the babe that was never hers...
the love that she craved never came...)
though lacking the ethereal ecstasy
her crystal shard of a heart nonetheless
broke
from the crushing lack of sleep
while the ticker tape parade
drew wide-eyed cringes
as one by one the gasps came
amplified by bells, whistles, and sirens
like a crowd at a horror flick
as metal birds speed with deadly
accuracy towards glass trees

darling, your emotional roboticism
is sterilizing you
sanitizing both the good and the bad
for you have flat-lined
you've reached the point of no return

there is no coming back from this one
no replay
no do-over
however, there is hope

a new door
new road
new journey
new destination

so, sacrifice that syringe of loss
for a plateful of destiny and
a chalice overflowing
with the light of better days
for it's neither feast nor famine
since these faces belong to the same
beast
superimposed
straining for airtime

it's your voice
hence your choice

we aren't victims of circumstance
or childhood romance
rock face clinging
while calamity howling
parental toxicity paired with
shamless duplicity

this is your death
your resurrection
your pendulum
swinging

Clarity

these glassy orbs modify
become momentarily transfixed
as I lose myself in the now -
aware
unaware

and the mind cools down
immersed in the sound
of tannin waters rumbling 'round
glacial boulders sculpted
(a '70s shag carpet stipple textured)

infinite pools drag me fathoms deeper
encasing me in a spherical chrysalid
where topside is muffled and muted and
where syncopated souls reside
out of phase
out of step
(neither out of tune
nor out of touch)
differentiating reality from
reality

processing information occurs partly
from perception of sensation but
processing emotion occurs in part
from perception of perception
(just to be clear)

hence, if I fail to be safely surface tethered
nested loops create down-filled duvet covers,
pillow-top mattresses,
crackling fireplaces,
and hot toddies
driving back February nor'easters

the real trick is not using
braided ropes but bungee cords

to snap you out of travelling
too far down
and now, come to think of it,
a spider's silken strand is ideal -
a tangential thread promising
freedom to enter and exit at will

no, I'm not advocating nonexistence,
escapism, meditative chanting,
or even withdrawal from life's
permanent web
but I am highly amenable and
susceptible to the dreamlike
purpose of mental permutations -
that psychological wave-function
bellowing out
"anything's possible!"

this metaphysical confluence
of Einstein, Rosen, Schwarzchild,
Heisenberg, Feynman, and many others
whose society laps at the edge
of some forgotten crescent beach
where stones are shadows
sand is diamond dust
and crystal trees shimmer as
much as fire opals once had

where men are not gods
but are children seeking questions
and questioning seekers while
finding unhinged answers every other day
that are clarified like fine wine, ghee,
and gold

these oysters open for those
who are willing to dive deep
and dive often
not gathering but tending
much as a farmer or shepherd would
by patiently and calmly labouring
so that when the time is just right

the plucky bivalves ascend and
lay at one's feet the most lustrous
string of pearls
formed not to wear but
only to behold
only to share

for by doling out dewdrops
to passersby who seek coats
to cast out winter's icy breath
their number diminishes not
because the having is in the giving
and wealth is measured by standards
of distribution
not accumulation

from this captivating flow
sinuous rills will follow
to which even the tone deaf
shall lend heavenly harmonious
voices

and the libretto's plain enough for all

Depth

so many of us mere surface beings
have acquired traits in the shallows

for example, without warning
Show and Tell becomes
a soapbox for showing off
(look at what I have!)
and for showing others up
(look at what I don't have...)

the vaults of these minds
remain devoid of cake
only plastered with an icy
soul-sickening sweetness

consequently, seeds lie dormant
for the lacking scent of water
and the dark crumbly feel of soil
while drivel falls from cracks
(gushing sometimes)
but you can't drink it without
choking
and neither boiling nor distillation
will it purify

yes, time marches deeper
into the dense thickets
and mountainous terrains
loom in the dusk
yet our diet brings only
sufficiency
(not satiety
not happiness)
for we continue feasting
on static while connections
weaken and fade
leaving what could have blossomed
into bright garden pathways

blocked up with tree-falls and
marshy sedges

true...
weeds do have practical uses
such as holding soil in place
while balancing its composition
but not in attracting the eyes
of the heart and holding its
attention

I am convinced that undiscovered lands
do exist in the Marianas Trench
of humanity
yet it appears (am I wrong?)
that the majority like where
the sharks prowl

recall how your skin tingled
with electrical excitement
while you strained to hear
the plop of stones dropped
down shafts as you counted
one-one thousand...
two-one thousand...
three-one thousand...
four-SPLOOSH!
and how you performed the trick
umpteen times with both hands
and both pockets filled while
giggling uncontrollably

these curious fears drive you
forward in fits and starts
through that cave mouth
like a novice with a stick shift
but you don't turn tail and run
for knowing is desired

no...

knowing is required

otherwise, what's it all for
anyway?

yes, the cats use the sandbox
across from loamy protozoan homes
but aren't mud pies simply too tasty
to leave behind?

these are the matters that forge us
into creatures who are much
bigger on the inside;
the necessary things
for growing angelic wings

only then will rivers start
babbling back baby talk to you
because you struggled to learn
their language

only then will the rocks permit you
a permanent seat -
an open invitation -
for you are determined to tread
carefully

only then will the tree people
reach out their arms and their
hands to embrace and breathe
life into your husk of a body
for you dared to call them friends

and only then shall no woodland
creature (either predator or prey)
look askance at your presence
with suspicion or guile

for you are the quiescent child
the deeper child
stretching beyond peace

Potential

see as I see

dragons spewing flowers
not flame
tornadoes building houses
not shattering them

see as I see

gold lining porticoes
not pockets
gems recalling beauty
not blood

see as I see

ideate for collaboration
not competition
borders are for gardens
not nations

see what will be

soon

Curtain Call

Thanks very much for choosing to read this book! Did it speak to you? Did it give you pause for a second thought? If you desire, please be so kind as to leave a rating and review.

Kindest regards,
Jason J. Humphreys

Other Books by Jason J. Humphreys

Sparks May Fly
The River Down the Road: selected poems

The Nicholsville Laureate

Please feel free to follow me on:

Amazon: https://www.amazon.com/author/jasonjhumphreys
Goodreads: https://www.goodreads.com/Hummerjay
Blogger: https://thenicholsvillelaureate.blogspot.ca
Pinterest: https://www.pinterest.ca/hummerjay53

www.ingramcontent.com/pod-product-compliance
Lightning Source LLC
Chambersburg PA
CBHW020605130626
46552CB00007B/3049